Permetrice Milroe Jackson

Rejoice AFTER REJECTION!

Rejoice After Rejection!

Dedication

This book is dedicated to some phenomenal women who have been supportive to me in the worst and the best of times. When I was disappointed, devastated and yes, even rejected, they listened to me, prayed for me and encouraged me in their own way. By the grace of God, I had the strength to stand some bitter experiences, but I lived to face blessed and better days! I'm grateful for your sisterhood and your friendship which are worth more than gold! In the words of Pastor Marvin Sapp, "I never would have made it, without you!" Many blessings to: My sisters, Linda Milroe and Trinette Milroe-Rowell; and to my God-sisters, Caroline Allen and Angeline Jackson.

I would also like to dedicate this to my brother, Quentin C. Milroe, my first male friend. Thank you for your continued encouragement through the years.

Permetrice

Acknowledgement

I appreciate my wonderful Mother, Gwendolyn Jolly Milroe who is the epitome of sophistication, grace, intelligence and perseverance. You showered me with a nurturing spirit that molded my life in an extraordinary way. You taught me lessons that have helped me navigate through life with a sure and solid foundation. I will be forever grateful for your boundless love and devotion to me and my siblings. You inspired me when you went back to school at the age of forty to earn your Bachelor's Degree in Art Education and taught in the Chicago Public Schools. You later earned a Master's Degree in Special Education and served in that field until you retired. Ironically, I followed your footsteps and I'm now an educator too. As I reflect on my childhood, I realize that you made life seem easy, as you juggled working, raising four children and taking care of our home. I actually thought we were wealthy, because we went to plays, movies, wonderful vacations and you dressed us from the finest department stores. I now know that we were simply part of the middle class, but we were richly loved. I thank God for blessing me with you as my mother. You will forever have my love and respect for all that you did and all that you do to positively impact my life!

Permetrice

Contents

Rejoice After Rejection!

Other Books by Permetrice Milroe Jackson:

Duplicity: Double Life Drama
A Novel

280 Pages of Suspense, Romance and Drama
Real Life, Real Talk
Available at Amazon.com (Kindle),
BarnesandNoble.com (Nook), Walmart.com,
Booksamillion.com and other online sites.
(Paperback and eBook)

Effective Prayers in Jesus's Name
Available at Amazon.com (Kindle),
BarnesandNoble.com (Nook),
ITunes.com/IBooks.com,
Bookamillion.com and other online sites.
(Paperback and eBook)

Introduction

What is rejection? Merriam Webster defines rejection as *to refuse to accept, consider or submit to; to refuse to receive; or to cast off.* Rejection is a natural occurrence in life as we navigate social friendships platonically and/or loving relationships. The normal rejections such as your peers not wanting you on their gym class team or a group not desiring you for their school club or clique are hurtful, but we all have experienced these minor offenses. This book will primarily focus on the type of rejection that occurs when you have experienced what you think is mutual love and respect in a monogamous, romantic relationship or a marriage. Unfortunately, you realized at some twisted point that the one you love has become nonchalant or cavalier towards you. Consequently, they may have been hostile with you and disconnected from you. Sadly, your sincere love was returned with confusing innuendos of belittlement, resentment or blatant disrespect.

If you are reading this and you know what I mean, continue to read. If not, read on anyway because the information and the included testimonies may help you one day to choose to triumph over a trial that the enemy of your soul, the devil wanted to use to discourage and destroy you. The devil wants you to give up after a devastating heartbreak, but victory can be yours as you choose to apply these practical principles in action concerning rejection, recovery and the ability to rejoice in your life.

No matter what you are going through right now, your present situation does not define who you are or what your destiny will be. Your current dilemma may have been allowed in your life, but it will not destroy you! Don't accept the negative comments that someone makes to you or that you hear from the "grapevine" about you. Know that you were wonderfully created by God and you have value. When you accept the horrible statements that a bully says to you as fact, you give that person too much power over you. That power can lead to influence that will potentially direct your path to a place that is contrary to your purpose and destiny! Why would you let an abusive individual steer you to their predetermined, erroneous location – for you?

When somebody belittles you, curses at you and blatantly disrespects you, they are not your friend! Run for your life! Detach, disengage and separate yourself from the foolishness that has become your everyday existence. They are being used as an instrument of the devil to discourage and destroy you. If you are married to a verbally abusive person, it's more complicated. Make sure to get advice from a wise minister, a pastor or a professional counselor to help motivate your spouse to change from being verbally abusive.

You were born full of purpose and God-given destiny. As you continue to walk with the Lord, he will get the glory out of your life. As you give God the glory, you get the good that flows back to earth over you. Please say this out loud, "God gets the glory out of my life and I get the great blessings!"

I interviewed various individuals who wanted to share their testimonies with you. Of course, the names have been omitted to protect the people involved. The stories are true, inspirational and meant to encourage you to know that you can heal and thrive after disappointment in relationships. Please realize that you are worth loving yourself enough to protect your sanity, peace of mind and safety. I wish you the best and God wants the best for you too. Please be assured that even after being rejected, there is a whole wonderful life to live, a destiny to fulfill and joy to envelope your journey! I am a witness that you truly can, **Rejoice After Rejection!**

Permetrice Milroe Jackson

Chapter 1
Leah's Loss and Blessings

There is an intriguing love story in the Bible of Jacob who wanted a wife and he traveled to Haran to find her **(Genesis 29)**. He met the beautiful Rachel by a well and fell in love with her. The custom of the day was to produce a large dowry to give to the family of the bequeathed so that the financial impact of the loss of a daughter would not be a hardship. Rachel's father Laban explained that the only way Jacob could have Rachel as his wife was to work on his land for seven long years. Laban even offered his older daughter Leah to Jacob, because it was customary for the older daughter to marry before the younger ones. Jacob basically said, *No, thank you!* He wanted Rachel.

Jacob agreed to pay the debt by working for the required seven years. At the conclusion of the agreed time of labor, he would be granted permission to marry the heart of his affection, Rachel. Just imagine his anticipated joy at the end of the labor-intensive commitment, long-awaited marriage ceremony and the consummation of his marriage to Rachel.

The Wedding Day

Think about how excited and happy Jacob must have been on his wedding day. He thought he was finally going to marry his beloved Rachel. With anticipation, the groom and the bride-to-be were each dressing in their own tents. The bride was being prepared; bathed, oiled down and perfumed to be joined to her husband.

After the meticulous preparations, the groom was in place, the minister was ready with the vows and the bride walked down the aisle. She was adorned with fabulous attire, she smelled wonderful and the cloth veil was draped about her face, properly concealing her features. The wearing of the veil symbolized the bride's virginity and purity. The couple took their marriage vows which represent the covenant relationship between a man and a woman that is blessed by God. Afterwards, the celebratory reception began. During that time, the bride's veil stayed in place throughout the entire event: therefore, Jacob did not suspect that anything deceitful was happening.

It was normal to eat lavish foods and drink wines during wedding receptions which the couple and their guests enjoyed. Everything seemed fine and Jacob felt that nothing could spoil his day. He had worked seven years for Rachel. She must have been one beautiful and special woman! Finally, Jacob walked his bride to the marriage tent and carried her inside. The sisters were identical in height and size and their speech had to be similar, because Jacob didn't notice that anything was wrong.

Jacob claimed his marital right to his bride and no doubt, whispered her name many times during their night of intimacy. I'm sure that sweet, romantic words were exchanged between the newlyweds. You may be wondering how Jacob was not able to see his wife's identity once the veil and clothing came off, but this was before modern electricity. The tent was dark. The next morning, the Bible says in **Genesis 29:25** that Jacob discovers the deceit of Laban, Rachel's father. He realizes that the woman he loves and for whom he had worked seven years, was not in his tent or his arms! The woman who he married and made love to was Leah, the "tender eyed," or who some Bible scholars call cockeyed or cross-eyed! Have you ever wondered why Leah didn't have a male admirer? It could be that Leah was rejected by Jacob and other men because of her appearance.

Sometimes we are rejected by people because of things we can't change such as our race, ethnicity, skin color, body type or other physical features. People may reject you, but you must learn to be accepting of yourself. You are unique and special! Improve what you can such as exercising to lose weight, tone up and increase your overall health, in-order-to become your best you. Remember to love and take great care of yourself through your journey to improvement.

Whatever the reason, Jacob didn't want or love Leah. He had asked to marry Rachel, but he inadvertently married Leah in an epic betrayal! Jacob had worked seven years with the desire in his heart to be Rachel's husband, but he had been tricked. What's ironic about this story is the background of Jacob, whose name means trickster or beguiler. Earlier in his life, Jacob with the help of his mother Rebekah, had deceived his father into giving him the birthright of his older brother Esau **(Genesis 27)**. Please know that you truly do reap what you sow, or as many people say, "What goes around, comes around!"

Jacob was frustrated and angry about the deceit of Laban and he resented Leah for her part in the deception. The Bible does not explain how Leah felt about being complicit in the betrayal, but we know that she willingly participated in the plan which was the only way it could have worked. That's right; Laban and Leah deceived Jacob!

Laban led Leah into lies and deceit.

Leah was a virtuous woman who worked on the family land. At some point, Leah was approached by her father with the idea of marrying Jacob even though she knew Rachel was engaged to be married to him. Although Leah assumed she would marry before her younger sister, apparently, no man was trying to marry her. She knew Jacob was in love with her sister Rachel, but she walked down that aisle anyway participating in the horrible deception. Leah didn't know how Jacob would handle the revelation of the deceit. She willingly married Jacob knowing he didn't love her. Leah not only deceived Jacob, but she betrayed her sister. By contributing to the deception, Leah took a very dangerous risk that ultimately, caused her to have a painful life of bitter rejection from her husband.

Before you judge Leah too harshly, let me ask you a question. How many times have you made a life changing decision that later produced a stressful trial of devastating disappointment, hurt and bitter rejection? Hopefully, as we look at Leah's painful life story, we will learn to make better decisions so that we are not exposed to a distressing situation that could have been avoided.

Remember, at the revelation that he had been tricked, Jacob became very angry. He looked for Laban and found him in the field. Jacob confronted Laban and questioned how he could dress up his older daughter and deceive him into saying vows to a woman that he had no intention of marrying. Laban let Jacob fuss and complain, but at the end of the conversation he told Jacob his only available option, which was unthinkable. Laban casually told Jacob that if he truly wanted to marry Rachel that he would have to work another seven years! Many men would have turned and walked away, but Jacob decided to work seven more years in order to marry his beloved Rachel. Can you imagine that? While married to Leah, Jacob's heart was still committed to the woman that he asked to marry, Rachel. His conversations and interactions with Leah were minimal. He merely tolerated Leah because he didn't want her. He wanted Rachel **(Genesis 29:30)**.

You can't make someone love you.

I can't imagine how this whole scenario affected Leah. Though Leah was part of the deception, she thought that in time, Jacob would grow to love her. Although Jacob continued to sleep with Leah, his heart wasn't toward her. He didn't love her. Leah was basically like the "other woman," used for her body without the true love from her husband.

During this time in Bible history, it was considered a blessing to have sons who would carry on the family name and help run the family business. Leah wanted to have children. She assumed that in due time, her husband would love her if she were to bare him sons. Leah prayed to conceive sons and the Lord opened her womb. She started giving birth to sons **(Genesis 29:31)**.

No matter what Leah cooked, in or out of the bedroom, no matter what she said to Jacob and no matter how many sons she had, Jacob did not return the love that she had for him. His heart was toward Rachel and he was working to have her hand in marriage. Leah was in a very disappointing, loveless marital relationship that was unimaginable. Though she was having sons that were a blessing to her, she still desired the love of her husband: but he loved her sister Rachel! After Leah gave birth to three sons, she was convinced that Jacob would finally love her. When he still didn't love her, she decided to just praise the Lord. She stated in **Genesis 29:35, "This time, I will praise the Lord!"** She even named their third son Judah, which means praise.

Even today, some women feel that if they get pregnant and have a baby that it will entrap or make a man stay and be committed to them. It didn't work for Leah and it usually does not work today. Children should be a blessed addition to a marital relationship that is already functioning well in a close bond of love and faithful commitment. They are not to be used for manipulative reasons.

We can learn from Leah's lessons and how she responded to the lack of love from her husband. In the middle of a battle, when you've done all you can do, take time to stop, pray and just give God the praise that is due him. You can't praise God and be depressed at the same time. Confuse the devil and get your praise on right in the middle of the madness and watch God turn your mourning into rejoicing! Change your sadness into joy knowing that the Lord is more than able to deliver you from any situation! Even while you are still in a difficult trial, God can give you peace in the storm, until your deliverance or change comes!

Just like Leah, sometimes you are being fruitful or successful in various areas of your life, but the main person you want to please may be unaware of or intentionally ignoring your best efforts! Their lack of appreciation towards you does not change the labor of love that you have done. Even if someone never recognizes your sacrifice, know that there is a God in Heaven that orders and records your life's steps. God will bless you and reward you above what you can imagine. We read in **Psalm 84:11 "…There is no good thing that the Lord will withhold from them that walk uprightly."** From this scripture, we can be confident that God will turn our negative situations around and richly bless us! Jesus said in **John 10:10, "…I came that you may have life and that more abundantly."** God truly cares about every area of your life. If your life is stagnant and at a negative point right now, it's not over. God will turn things around in your favor, right on time!

Leah may not have had the love from her husband that she desired, but she repented for her deceitful actions against Jacob. We know this, because God had mercy on her. God forgave Leah and favored her, allowing her to have many children whom she adored. This lets me know that even when you make mistakes, there is hope for redemption. You must repent or be sorry for your sins and wrong actions before God and change your ways. To truly repent means to turn from the sins that you were committing and stop doing them! Then, God will have mercy on you, forgive you and bless you.

God's Grace and Mercy…

The important truth to remember is that God gives us the chance to get our life in order. As long as you are alive and have a humble heart, ask God for forgiveness and stop willfully sinning, God will have mercy on you and forgive you. By his grace and with his power and authority, he will turn your life around and bless you according to his perfect will. Thank God for his grace and mercy!

The Bible says in, **1 John 1:9, "If we confess our sins, he is faithful and just to forgive us our sins, and cleanse us from all unrighteousness."** The Bible contains scriptures that provide guidance and teaching for improving your moral character. It explains the way you should live and offers help for you to truly walk uprightly with God. These principles are what the Christian lifestyle is all about. Be determined to have a deeper relationship with the Lord. Your spiritual growth and maturity will develop by: praying to God every day; praising him for who he is and for his goodness; trusting him through the process and journey of life; learning his word through reading the Bible and faithfully attending church services; and living each day to your fullest potential. Let every day be an opportunity to learn and grow in God so that you become a better person and a true example of a child of God.

Jesus was also rejected.

Jesus never sinned and spent his life helping people, but he was also rejected! Although Jesus healed the sick, raised the dead, restored sight to the blind, fed the hungry, delivered folk who were possessed with devils and performed other miracles, he was rejected by the religious folk; the Pharisees and the Sadducees. There were common people and some in authority who doubted that he was the Son of God despite his teachings, authority and anointed ministry. Since he was rejected, we know there will be times that we will suffer rejection. We must realize who we are in Christ, what our destiny is and continue to pursue purpose.

Some people will be jealous of the anointing on your life, but they don't know what you have suffered in the past. The anointing cost something! God anoints you for the purpose and calling on your life, so it is foolish to envy someone's anointing. Other individuals were not meant to stay in your life, because your destiny is greater than their narrow vision for you! They could have delayed you, warring against your calling. God did you a favor removing them, because their cantankerous actions were toxic to your great destiny! When you know who you are and the assignments that you are to work on and accomplish for you, your family and the Kingdom of God, you will become a powerful voice to be heard and an anointed vessel to be honored. Praise God for delivering you from dead-weight relationships!

Chapter 2
Rachel's Trials and Triumphs

Rachel knew Jacob loved her, so she patiently waited to marry him. Just imagine how hurt Rachel must have felt knowing that Jacob would unknowingly marry her sister Leah. Rachel had to quietly sit in her tent as the wedding ceremony took place knowing that night, Jacob would make love to her sister! Later, she watched as her sister carried babies and birthed sons. These sisters had negative feelings toward each other because of the betrayal. They also envied each other. Rachel was envious that Leah was married to Jacob and she was conceiving and birthing sons. Leah was envious of Rachel because Jacob loved Rachel and not her. Leah and Rachel envied each other because each sister wanted what the other one had.

This was a dysfunctional family dynamic of betrayal, secrets, envy and rejection! I believe that this mixed-up family situation is included in the Bible to clearly show us that it is better to live a life of integrity than to participate in trickery and deceit to get what or who does not belong to you! We can learn from their story, because bad life decisions have the potential to damage you and your family.

I must address the issue of envy. Envy does not solve problems, because it makes you focus on what others have and what you perceive as lack in your life. This can make you feel miserable and hinder your progress toward your dreams. You should be thankful for your current blessings and continue to move forward by working on what you desire to have in your life. In **James 2:14** we find, **"Faith without works is dead."** Pray and believe, but keep working on your dreams. In time, you will achieve your goals and earn your reward.

Rachel finally gets her husband.

Eventually, Jacob married Rachel, but she was barren or unable to conceive a child. When Rachel saw that she could not have children, she envied her sister, because Leah was fertile and had no problem getting pregnant. Leah was conceiving sons while Rachel was childless and depressed. Frustrated, Rachel said to Jacob in **Genesis 30:1, "Give me children or I shall die!"** Rachel was desperate to conceive a baby. In ancient Israel, a woman was considered blessed by God if she had many children and Rachel didn't have any.

Rachel prayed about her barrenness and asked God to bless her with children. God finally opened her womb allowing her to conceive and become a mother.

Sometimes situations like this happen in your life. You may see someone who is prospering in the same area of your desired dreams, but you have not been able to achieve success. You may feel like your blessing is taking too long, but God has a scheduled or appointed time for your dreams to manifest or come to fruition. The Bible says in **Psalm 31:15, "My times are in your hands;…"** In this scripture, the word "times" in the Hebrew is **eth** which is interpreted to mean, **"Due Season"** so be encouraged. Whatever dream(s) you are working on, whether it is a great promotion in your career, starting a business, launching a ministry, publishing a book, writing and publishing music, having a professional singing career or any other dreams, know that your Due Season is on the way! In other words, God knows your heart's desire and what he has destined for you to do. When it is the right time for you to accomplish your dreams, you will have success in those areas that he has purposed for you! Just like God opened Rachel's womb and allowed her to be fruitful and have children, he is going to allow you to birth the "baby" that you are working on!

As a result of the deceit of Laban and Leah and their dysfunctional family structure, the children were affected. Think about the chaotic relationships between the half-brother and sister/cousins who had mothers who were married to the same man? I know… It's too much to process. Clearly, this was not God's best for them.

Have you ever had a love relationship or marriage that was not working out, causing you excessive stress and unnecessary heartache? Maybe it could have been avoided had you prayed diligently and waited on God's direction and best answer for you. Compromising your worth and marrying the wrong spouse may open you up to sorrow, tears, depression and possible abuse. Please care for yourself enough to believe that you deserve mutual love, affection and commitment from your true mate. When God blesses you with your true soul mate, your marriage will be peaceful and happy. Your children will have the benefit of a loving, stable environment to develop into all they were intended to be.

When hostility is prevalent between a couple in the home, children suffer needlessly. Kids are emotionally damaged when they see one parent disrespected and victimized either verbally or physically by the other parent. Sometimes they internalize the conflict they see and think that the parental problems are somehow caused because of them. That negative, dysfunctional family environment has the potential to mentally harm children causing them to struggle to establish and maintain normal, healthy relationships later in life. This is especially true if they don't get counseling to help them process their feelings, recover and heal. Children need a peaceful, safe, loving and stable environment to ensure their positive moral, social and emotional development. They may see drama on television or in a movie at the theater. They do not need to see drama played out in your home!

Chapter 3
Break the cycle of abuse!

Marriage is such a special and significant relationship that you need to pray about who you should marry and have children with. One person's unresolved emotional baggage, perhaps from a hostile home-life from their childhood can create a barrage of broken hearts and wounded lives with generational repercussions. Many times, hurt people make the choice to hurt other people in their life. Break the cycle of abuse! Don't just pray about your spousal choice, but wait for God to answer you before you attach your heart, soul and life to somebody who is wrong for you. The incorrect mate may have been sent from the devil to divert or delay your real destiny. If you marry a person who is less than God's best for you, that decision can create unnecessary chaos in your life. Please read the following testimony from a precious woman who unfortunately, failed to diligently pray before getting married. Had she only prayed and listened to God, her life would have been different.

Marriage Mayhem...

I dated a man in college who appeared to have his life in order. We met in the school's Christian Fellowship and started to quickly form a friendship that led to a relationship. We often ate together in the cafeteria or we rode the local bus to different restaurants downtown. We shared the same faith, prayed and studied the Bible together. Before a year had passed, we were discussing marriage. When talking about Heaven one day, he mentioned that he could not imagine a place being so wonderful that it would be better than living with me in marriage. Yes, he had some wonderful lines that I fell for, hook, line and sinker.

Beyond the great friendship that we shared, we spent a lot of quality time together. We would rise early to jog around the campus and the surrounding community to get our exercise in. We attended a local church on Sundays and he often quoted Scriptures from the Bible implying that he believed the Word of God and practiced what he heard preached. We set a date to marry and I started planning a beautiful wedding. Everything that he said, his loving actions and the gentle way that he treated me convinced me that he would be a loving and supportive husband. I was all in.

I was young chronologically and young in the Lord, but God tried to give me a warning. One day, I got what I now know was a check in my spirit that I should pray to God about if this man was my true mate. As I bowed my head to pray, I was fearful that the Lord was going to say, 'No; he is not the one for you.' There was one side of me that didn't understand this subtle, but wise warning from the Spirit of God. The other side of me was confused to even question my fiancée's integrity because he seemed to only have Godly characteristics and strong Christian values. Unfortunately, I ignored the feeling that I had that he may not be "the one" for me.

Though he was not, I was still a virgin and we decided to do things God's way and wait until we were married to have sex. He appeared to be the perfect man for me. I didn't pray, but I assumed that surely, everything was going to be great after we got married. Our relationship felt right; therefore, I made the decision based on my feelings.

The wedding day arrived, and we said our vows before God, family and friends. I believed that we would live happily-ever-after, or so the fairytales go. I was so wrong.

*My husband immediately changed. Within one week, he started treating me mean like he didn't love me or want me. Conversely, other times he acted like he cared. His mind and emotions seemed to vacillate from day to day. What was this? I didn't make him marry me! This man was unstable. He was the epitome of what the Bible says in **James 1:8, "A double-minded man is unstable in all of his ways."** You may want to know how devastating of a blow that was to me. It was horrible.*

I was so private and independent that I didn't feel like I could share what I was going through with anyone. I thought that I just had to stay right there, pray and be the best wife that I could be. I felt that I had to somehow make lemonade out of the lemons that I was dealt. I really stayed too long, because you can't make anyone do anything that they are unwilling to do. I was in a tortured nightmare that would last for over two decades. It was a loveless and miserable marriage. My husband was verbally, mentally and eventually physically abusive. He was not only abusive, but he also led a double life and started cheating on me with (admittedly), at least seven different women! He was not loving, faithful, supportive or committed to me. He was not a good or attentive father to our children. I finally made the decision to divorce my tormentor.

I truly believe our union was a terrible mistake. I wonder what my life would have been like if I had only diligently prayed about marrying him. I know the Lord would have shown me that this man was not the best for me. If I had prayed and listened to God, I would have avoided a marriage full of pain, disappointment and emotional and physical abuse. I now realize the importance of seeking God about such an important, life-changing decision. God's best mate for me would have loved me as Christ loves the church **(Ephesians 5:25)**. *He would have cherished the gift that I was and he would have valued his marriage and family. I'll never marry anyone again without seeking the Lord's will and listening for His answer. Now I value who I am in Christ and I want the best man that the Lord has for me. I now seek the Lord for answers in all areas of my life. With God's help, I have healed from the trauma that my ex-husband caused me. I was tormented, but now I'm free!*

F. W.

Double-minded Dilemmas

The above testimony is tragic, but also an inspirational story. It's sad because the woman married a man without seeking God only to discover that her husband was deceitful and like a wolf in sheep's clothing. While dating, he quoted the Bible, went to church, prayed with her and made her feel satisfied that he was saved and serving God like she was. In the end, he simply played the role that he knew she needed to see to convince her to marry him. Her husband was not only deceitful, but mean-spirited. I believe he will have to give an account to God for the way in which he mistreated his wife and family. Clearly, he was double-minded; therefore, he was not God's best for her. Before deciding on who to marry, which is a wonderful life-changing experience, you should diligently seek the Lord. The Bible says in **Proverbs 3:6, "In all your ways, acknowledge me and I will direct your path."**

God knows the intent of an individual's heart; therefore, he knows the future actions of that person. That's why it is critical that you pray and seek God before agreeing to marry someone. After praying, wait for God's answer. Make sure to seek wise counsel by attending pastoral or other professional pre-marital counseling. You truly owe it to yourself to ensure that your mate is stable and fully aware of the serious and very special, covenant relationship that God designed marriage to be. We find in **Hebrews 13:4, "Marriage is honorable in all and the bed undefiled; but whoremongers and adulterers God will judge."** God wants you to enjoy and be blessed by the love, fidelity and commitment that comes from being joined in holy matrimony to a dedicated spouse. Marriage is a covenant union that is blessed by God. In fact, the first institution that God established was marriage between Adam and Eve in the Garden of Eden. The bottom line is: Marriage is for grown folks who desire to love and support their life-long mate sincerely, lovingly and faithfully.

Chapter 4
Words are Powerful!

There was a cliché years ago that said, 'Sticks and stones may break my bones, but words will never hurt me.' Many people quoted this, but was it true? I submit to you that words have the power to hurt or heal. Words may not harm you physically, but they can leave bruises emotionally and scar an individual mentally. Words are very powerful! You should always take care in how you communicate with others. Be cognizant of what declarations or words that you say over your own life and your loved ones. Once negative words leave your mouth, it's hard to retract them: therefore, think before you speak. Don't blurt out words in anger that you will regret later. Handle another person's feelings as gentle as you would a precious child. The Bible says in **Proverbs 18:21, "Life and death are in the power of the tongue.** Words are so potent that they have the ability to create actions, good or bad. In other words, negative words can lead to negative actions. Fortunately, positive words can lead to positive actions. Learn to speak in a positive manner and deposit uplifting words of life to others!

Please read the following testimony of a woman who suffered verbal abuse from her husband, who claimed to love her. According to his wife, he was an excellent financial provider, but he lacked an understanding of marital love, compassion and sympathy. According to his wife, this man was not emotionally supportive to her and he constantly attacked her sense of self-worth. That is unfortunate. He didn't honor or respect her as his wife or fulfill his duty in the home of being a true husband and loving father. Apparently, this man was very selfish. He probably should have stayed single.

He was as mean as a rattlesnake.

I married the love of my life and thought we would enjoy a lifetime of happiness and fulfillment. Unfortunately, I was wrong. Almost immediately after we got married, our happy home turned into a war zone. My husband became negative and hostile towards me. He complained about almost everything that I did. He loved the taste of my food, but he complained about my choice of food to cook. He didn't like the way I vacuumed the floor or the way that I cleaned the house. Not only was he a habitual complainer, he became verbally abusive calling me names and routinely disrespecting me. This continued even after we had children. My self-esteem dropped to a very low level and I became depressed. He eventually resorted to some physical violence which I had always said that I would never tolerate. We went to get help through pastoral counseling and he stopped hitting me, but he continued to verbally attack me. He also neglected me and our children by emotionally withdrawing and refusing to spend quality time with us. When I could not take the mistreatment any longer, I separated from him and eventually, I divorced him. Ironically, even though he didn't treat me lovingly or with respect, he didn't want the divorce. I guess he enjoyed being mean to me and distant from us as a family. I felt that he would never change since through the years, I had given him every opportunity to treat me the right way, but his behavior got worse. Unfortunately, my marriage ended. To keep my sanity, I chose to be free from an abusive, duplicitous man.

A. O.

What a dirty, rotten shame…

The above testimony was from a woman who was abused both verbally and physically by a man who should have loved and respected her. He rejected her love and every effort that she made to please him. Although it's sad that a marriage ended, and a family was divided, this wife felt that she had to get out of an abusive marriage for her mental health and physical safety. Fortunately, she later had sessions from a therapist to help her heal and recover from her tormentor's hostile treatment; therefore, restoring her self-esteem. She reported that her children were also helped by a trained child therapist. It is important to pray, but it is also appropriate to get specialized, professional counseling as needed. That is just wise advice and it can help you recover from traumatic experiences.

Beware of the mean, manipulative bully!

What drives a person to constantly speak negatively or abusively to another person that they vowed to love and cherish in marriage? What could be their possible motive? Have you ever been on the receiving end of such brutal verbal attacks? How do you respond when somebody verbally assaults you? Is your first response to strike back with as much venom as possible? Is your goal to give the attacker a "piece of your mind?" I submit to you that an individual who finds it necessary to speak to you in a negative and hostile manner is an abusive person and perhaps a narcissist.

A narcissist is overly self-involved. He or she feels superior to you and wants all credit and compliments for themselves. Even when you've done a great job, a narcissist will attempt to take all the credit while dismissing you and your efforts as miniscule. Hurling insults your way seems to motivate the narcissistic person to inflict more pain towards you, especially when they see that it bothers you. They may even make outlandish accusations about you that you both know are false and ridiculous. This type of person is mean-spirited and they have a twisted need to belittle you to make themselves feel empowered. If you find yourself involved with this type of person, it's important to dismiss their negative comments from your mind. What another individual negatively says about you is not who you are. You are better than their small summation of you. Fortunately, the words of a verbally abusive person do not define who you are nor do those horrible words determine where God is taking your life. Those individuals have a spirit of control, and they want total authority over your life. They want to manipulate you in an unhealthy way. The good news is, God is in control and he has the final say in your life!

Don't believe the lies of the enemy!

God has a divine purpose for you and you are special in his eyes. The Bible says in **Psalm 139:14, "I praise you because I am fearfully and wonderfully made; your works are wonderful, I know that full well."** Stop listening to someone's ugly comments about you. Don't digest them, process them or take ownership of anything that is limited, derogatory or demeaning. You are not what you've been through or what you're currently going through! Do not believe nor embrace the negative images that others paint of you or accept the ugly statements as the truth. Start believing what God says about you, because you are who God says you are!

Start declaring the blessings of Abraham over your life! God promised to bless Abraham and his seed and we are the seed of Abraham according to **Genesis 22:18**. Make the decision to speak with positive words and a voice of victory! You are strong and able to pursue your purpose with determination to fulfill your destiny. The

Bible says in **Jeremiah 29:11, "I know the thoughts I have towards you; thoughts of peace and not of evil to give you an expected end."** God has specific thoughts and great plans for your life that will give glory to him and bring joy and fulfillment to you. Practice speaking blessings and prosperity over your life, because as we have already reviewed according to **Proverbs 18:21, "Life and death are in the power of the tongue."** Speak life and encouraging declarations about yourself and others. These wonderful and up-lifting words are persuasive and powerful. They become your positive confessions or Verbal Victories! I have included some examples of affirmations and scriptures that you can say out loud as you recover and heal from the bitter pain of rejection. They are also great at any time, because they are optimistic and inspirational. These positive Verbal Victories will help feed your soul with life-enriching spiritual food that will strengthen you!

As you motivate yourself with these scriptures, declarations and your genuine belief in what you are saying, you will positively change and become better. Make the decision to agree with the wonderful destiny that God has planned for you. Continue walking on your God-given journey in life and get all that God has intentionally designed, just for you!

Verbal Victories: Confessions to Overcome Rejection

I am who God says I am! I am blessed, healed and delivered to make a difference in this world!

"I know the thoughts or plans that I have for you; Thoughts of peace and not of evil to give you an expected end."
Jeremiah 29:11

"I can do all things through Christ who strengthens me."
Philippians 4:13

"No weapon that is formed against me shall prosper."
Isaiah 54:17

Though man may reject me, God sees me as the apple of his eye.
Psalm 17:8

I forgive those who have harmed me, I forgive myself for my mistakes and the sins of my past and reach for my goals! I am forgiven!

"…Forgetting those things that are behind, I press toward the mark of the high calling of God through Christ Jesus."
Philippians 3:13

"I am fearfully and wonderfully made; … I know full well."
Psalm 139:14

Though I have suffered; I'm strong, saved and settled in God!

"…Weeping may endure for a night, but joy comes in the morning."
Psalm 30:5

Chapter 5
Lost Love, Lessons Learned

One of the most painful forms of rejection is when a love relationship, especially a marriage suddenly changes and you are cast aside as if you and your heart are simply characters from the pages of a fictional story. Please read the following testimony from a woman who was broken hearted by a man to the point where she literally wanted to end her own life. No matter how devastated you feel, suicide is not the answer! You will survive your heart-breaking dilemma. I praise and thank the Lord that this woman didn't take her life!

Love God and yourself enough to live!

I left a store one day and was greeted by a handsome man who struck up a conversation with me. There was something special about him that intrigued me. He asked me for my number and I gave it to him. Our first telephone conversation lasted for hours. He asked me out and we connected almost immediately. We became a couple and I was one happy woman, because he treated me like a queen. He was a gentleman; very loving, supportive and my best friend. He introduced me to his parents and his entire family. We dated for five and a half years and we were inseparable. It sounds unreal, but we never argued, nor did we have any break-ups. He asked me to marry him, but wanted to get the approval from my parents. He first approached my mother and she said it would be fine with her if that was what we wanted to do. He then asked my father for my hand in marriage. We were so happy.

Abruptly, one day while I was thinking about and planning our pending wedding, he came by to say that he could not see me anymore. What? We didn't have any problems. He stopped calling me and taking me out on dates. He was gone. He didn't give a reason why he didn't want to see me anymore or explain his actions. Overnight, I had to adjust to being without the love of my life. Since we had been intimate, I missed making love to him and the closeness that we shared. I was devastated! I went into a deep depression which led to me having suicidal thoughts. During this time, I lived in a country town with my parents and I knew that my father had a shotgun. One day while home alone, I became very distraught; crying and shaking. I believe I was on the verge of a nervous breakdown. I decided to go to my father's closet where he kept the weapon. I took the gun out and loaded it with bullets; ready to take my life. Suddenly, it was as if I heard the voice of God speaking in my spirit. He told me, "Daughter, if you will serve me, I'll lift your burdens!" I said "Yes Lord." I felt something disconnect from me. It started at my toes and I felt it crawling up through my body. It came out through my chest. I looked up to see where it went because it felt so real. It actually felt like my chest opened up releasing it out of me. God later revealed to me that it was a demonic, suicidal spirit that he snatched out, delivering me! Instantly, I knew God had done something for me because the burden was lifted! I knew I was set free and I felt better! Though I was raised in church, I didn't personally know the Lord. God saved and delivered me that day in my parents' house!

It is a miracle that I didn't commit suicide. I thank God that he intervened and encouraged me away from my place of insane, suicidal thoughts. I'm alive because God loved me enough to give me a reason to live. The Lord Jesus Christ came into my heart, saved my soul and he gave me the strength to go on. He gave me the power to walk alone and he healed my broken heart. God took all of the pain away. I wanted to share my story to help someone else who may be like I was; about to give up and die. Do not harm or kill yourself. God loves you and he will bless you with the right person when the time is right. Take care of your emotions and live your life.

Pastor M. A., Macon, GA

The devil is still the father of lies!

The above testimony was from a lady who has now become a powerful Woman of God! She is a living miracle, because she defied the odds and moved from a place of despondency to living a full and accomplished life. What the devil meant to be evil, by tempting her to commit suicide, God has made it good for her and many other people like her. God totally turned her life around. He has allowed her to be a friend to many people and a mentor to ministers! She does not have natural children, but she has spiritual sons and daughters. God has blessed her to be a blessing to many people.

To those who are depressed and suffering just like this lady was hurting from a devastated broken heart, know that you can make it. God loves you! I know that you may be in pain and the heartache is real, but the reality is that things are not as bad as they appear. I have a saying that, "The devil will paint a mental picture that is better than a Picasso, but it is a lie from the pit of hell!" Don't give up on life based on a challenging dilemma! Life is worth living and you will survive the bitter storm of rejection!

The following testimonial is from a woman who fell in love with a worldly man and started living with him. He promised to marry her, but he kept breaking his promise. God delivered a message to her, but she didn't listen to the message. Please learn from her mistake the lessons of being obedient to God, walking in his divine will and waiting for the right person to be your life-long mate in marriage.

God gave the answer, but she didn't listen.

When I met who would become my second husband, I fell in love, but subconsciously, I realized he was not the man for me. I found out too late that his motive to hook-up with me was very different from mine. Although he was four years my junior, that was ok because age is nothing, but a number. I had always dated younger men, so that wasn't an issue for me. The main issue was that he saw that I was well established with a good job, my own home and a nice car. He thought that he would be able to use me.

That was his initial reason for dating me, however, the longer we dated and he got to know me, he fell in love with me.

As time progressed, I realized that he was a womanizer and therefore, unfaithful. Several times he told me that women were his weakness. He was tall, dark and handsome and women were spell-bound by his good looks and charisma. He was built like a body builder and he dressed like a model on the cover of a GQ magazine. I must confess, I was also spell-bound. Some research suggests that when we look for a mate, we look for someone who reminds us of our father. Truth be told, I did this with him, because he looked like and dressed just like my dad who was deceased. Unfortunately, he reminded me of my father in another way, because my father was also a womanizer. Regrettably, I was attracted to the wrong type of men for most of my life.

One day, my girlfriend invited me to a Christian Tent Meeting with a guest minister who operated with a very powerful, prophetic gift. The man of God preached a message and afterwards, he asked if anyone wanted him to pray for them. I immediately went up for prayer.

*As the Prophet started praying for me, I was shocked by what he was telling me, from the Lord. I knew this man was a true prophet of God because everything that he told me was true and no one knew but me, my fiancé and God! By the Spirit of God, he literally saw right inside of my house that I shared with my fiancé! I shouted and ran around the tent because I knew I had to end my relationship with my fiancé. I wanted to be obedient to God, because the Bible says in **1 Samuel 15:22**, **"…obedience is better that sacrifice."** I knew I had to sacrifice my relationship by ending it and obeying my Lord and Savior. One* *thing that the Man of God said was that, 'I had been given many broken promises of marriage.' He also stated that 'the man I was with was not my husband and that the Lord had a Spirit-filled man who would be my husband.' On the way home that night, my friend who had invited me to the tent service confirmed that according to the prophetic word that had come forth, the man that I loved and lived with, was not who God wanted me to marry.*

When I got home that night, I began to tell my fiancé what the Man of God had prophesied to me. He was troubled by what I shared with him and he said, "I'm scared because that man doesn't sound like me." I told him, "It could be you, if you would just yield your heart and give your life to Christ." I was ready to reluctantly walk away from the relationship even though I wanted to marry him. Eventually, my fiancé asked me to marry him again. I was hesitant, but I prayed about it. Without waiting to hear from God, I said "YES!" I hoped that I wasn't being disobedient to God, because my fiancé had started going to church. I convinced myself that he was my blessing from God. He wasn't.

Unfortunately, our marriage didn't last 2 months; we separated. For many years we tried to mend this broken marriage. It was impossible for it to work, because my husband was a habitual cheater and he could not be trusted. Eventually, we divorced. I was so in love with him that I was hurt and distraught over the divorce. I never forgot about that prophesy given to me under the tent. I should have never married that man, because God had spoken. He was not the right man for me. After he finally wanted to marry me and insisted on getting married, I thought he would change. He didn't want to lose me, but he also wanted other women. Sometimes we just need to walk away from a relationship no matter how much we love a person, because in the end, you will be hurt and disappointed. If God did not ordain a marriage and if it is not build on Godly principles, it will not stand. I've learned from my mistakes and never want to make the same ones again. At this point I have not remarried; however, I'm waiting on God for the right person.

J. M., Atlanta, GA

Guard your heart!

This was an unfortunate situation where this woman suffered for years. She loved that man and gave her precious heart to him even though the Lord had clearly stated that he was not her husband. She was entangled in a love affair where she had a soul-tie to an ungodly man. Since she was already living with him and sleeping with him, her judgment was clouded by love, lust and an emotional roller-coaster from the infidelity that he was committing. The extra women that he was seeing made it impossible for him to properly bond with and be faithful to his wife. His choices, sins and actions damaged her self-esteem. She was devastated and depressed for years after their divorce.

Your heart is too precious to give to an individual that refuses to love, honor and respect you. Again I say, guard your heart!

Prayer is Key!

No matter how much you love someone, seek the Lord by praying about whether they are your correct mate. Again, I say PRAY. Wait for God's answer. Then, once the Lord gives you your answer, obey Him. If you are with God's best mate for you, make sure to get advice and pre-marital counseling from a respected pastor, minister or professional marriage counselor. This proactive investment of your time will help ensure that both people know the serious and special relationship that marriage is meant to be. Sound, wise advice will also help you understand the roles of being a supportive, mature mate and it would create positive and realistic expectations for a happy and fulfilled marriage.

If the Lord shows you that the person you are dating is not for you, separate yourself from the person immediately. God knows what's best for you. He knows the true heart of a person. Though it may hurt initially, in the long run, the pain of separating would be much less than marrying the wrong person and subjecting yourself to a lifetime of turmoil and ultimately, bitter rejection.

Marrying the wrong person not only may subject you to neglect and further rejection, but that mate may go against the marital covenant and commit adultery. When a man or woman chooses to have extra-marital affairs, they are also choosing to betray and neglect their spouse. These actions are not only painful, but they are dangerous! People who habitually choose to commit adultery are living a very duplicitous lifestyle. An unfaithful spouse's lifestyle increases the risk of exposure to sexually transmitted diseases (STDs) to both people. They could not only get an STD that's treatable, but they could possibly infect themselves and their spouse with a disease that's incurable! Living that kind of promiscuous lifestyle is just reckless behavior. It is sad that individuals destroy their reputation and devastate family units in such an irresponsible manner.

I want to advise single individuals to examine yourself and be honest in your self-assessment. If you don't have the maturity and discipline to be faithful and monogamous in a marriage, don't get married! Don't mess over someone's life! As I've stated before, marriage is for grown, mature and committed people who are willing to give and receive in a covenant bond of marital bliss, in a lifelong love relationship!

Chapter 6
Real Mothers Love

The final testimony is a touching story of a woman who was rejected by her birth mother! It is sad to me, because I was truly loved by my mother and my father. I know the awesome responsibility and boundless joy of being a devoted mother. I can't imagine rejecting any of my children. Unfortunately, this woman's story is not as rare as you may think. Fortunately, she survived the bitter rejection and she became a great mother. She had to maximize the moments and the love that was given to her from other people that God placed in her life. It is great to know that even though people may fall short and choose to operate in a dysfunctional manner toward us, God always provides what we need. Please read the following story and be inspired to be your best self in all your relationships.

"God Loves the Little Children"

I was conceived as a result of an adulterous affair by my father who was married and my mother. In our society, some consider you to be a bastard or an illegitimate person. Thank God that he loves us, no matter how we were conceived. It's never the child's fault. In my case, it was the lusting affair of two adults who made bad decisions.

I was the apple of God's eye and my entire family. Well, maybe not the entire family. You see, my mother refused to raise me. I was raised by my maternal grandparents, my aunts and my uncle. Ironically, although my Father was married, and the affair hurt his wife, my step-mother accepted me with loving arms. I loved her as much as she loved me, until her death. Unfortunately, I never had or felt loved by my biological mother even until this day.

Years ago, I tried to get answers, so I wrote my mother a seven-page letter. I needed to know why she did not love me and why she treated me as though I wasn't her daughter. I've had so many failed love relationships and bitter rejections, that I felt I wasn't worthy of love. After all, I felt if my mother didn't love me, how could anyone else love me? I always thought that a mother was supposed to nurture, protect, teach and love you, but since I never received that from my biological mother, I thought I wasn't worthy of love. Please don't think I didn't have love from others in my life, because I did. My grand-parents, uncle, aunts, father and step-mother loved me unconditionally. You might say, wasn't that enough love? Yes, it was, but there was still a missing void in my life. I was missing that maternal love. The bond a mother normally develops with her growing child in the womb and the connection of the umbilical cord is unique. The bond and the love usually grows even after the cord is cut. My mother and I never developed a bond.

My mother never acknowledged getting the letter that I sent her: therefore, she never answered the many questions I presented to her. A reliable source in our family confirmed that she received my letter, but she never talked to me about it. I have forgiven my mother for rejecting me, but I still feel the void of her withheld love and affection. God has loved me in-spite of my dysfunctional relationship with my birth mother. God said in **Hebrews 13:5-6, "He will never leave me or forsake me."** *I know that I am safe in his arms. God is a Father to the fatherless and a Mother to the motherless. I love Him, as He loves me! God gave me a heart to love everyone, especially children. I don't like to see kids abused or mistreated. I have a very special relationship with my son and grandson. I love them to life. Just as Jesus gave his life for me and you, I would lay down my life for my son and grandson. That's real love and I'm a real mother!*

J. M., Atlanta, GA

God always provides what we need!

The above testimony was from a woman who was devastated by the rejection from her birth mother who refused to love her or raise her. She was hurt by her mother's negligence and cold attitude towards her. Rejection can be passed down generationally, but fortunately, this woman didn't reject her own sons. She was also rejected and hurt by men whom she loved, but who rejected her. By the grace of God and over time, she has been healed from these horrible experiences of rejection. She was emotionally healed and God will heal you too!

Chapter 7
The Choice to Rejoice

The various testimonies in this book are all true and emotionally touching to read, but hopefully they will help inspire somebody who has gone through a similar situation. I'm so grateful to the contributors who were willing to share their stories in order to encourage others to know they are not alone and that they can survive through any kind of heartbreak or relationship rejection.

Did you ever ask, "Why me?"

You may have asked the question, "Why me, Lord?" Well, I have a question for you, "Why not you?" Sometimes we go through hard times because of our own choices: however, other times we go through various trials for our development and God's Kingdom purpose. It may be because you are anointed for a special purpose. While salvation is a gift from God, the anointing cost something! Let me explain. The difficult trials that you experience are packed with purpose to help develop you into who you are to be and to equip you with what you need to accomplish your assignments in the earth. Have you ever wondered why you start meeting people who are going through a trial that you already experienced and successfully made it through it? Dear people, that's no coincidence. Your trials develop and strengthen you, but they also help you be a blessing to other people. When you share your experience and how you made it through it with somebody else that is dealing with the same or similar problem, you encourage them to press through the bitterness of rejection, or any other trial. Your testimony can encourage them to continue to live so that they can share their story. God never allows a trial without a good reason. Rest assured that if God allows it in your life, he always has lessons for you to learn and a specific purpose in mind. Pass the test and gain a powerful testimony!

God has confidence in your strength!

What? Sometimes, there are negative events that happen in life that seem to knock the wind out of you. There are trials that linger past their assumed expiration date. You may have been slapped with a lawsuit or literally slapped by a person who was always gentle with a kind soul, but suddenly he or she became violent. Maybe you received a doctor's report that was not favorable and you're standing in need of a miracle healing.

No matter what you face, know that God has already equipped you with what you need to make it through the difficult times. God promised that he would not put more on you than you are able to handle. Please be assured that God knows you and he has already evaluated your level of strength; therefore, your trial is measured according to your ability to make it through it! In other words, God knows the amount of Word that your soul and spirit have absorbed through teaching, personal study and experience as well as your level or measure of faith in him. Based on this revelation, when you are hollering out to God saying, "I can't take anymore!" God is watching you, knowing what is in you and declaring, "Yes, you can. I've already evaluated you." What? Yes. God has more confidence in you, than you have in yourself. If the trial is still going on, know that there is a reason and it is only for a set season or time. Realize that God's got you! He will ensure that you get the maximum, spiritual growth, the intended lesson and the testimony to share with others, because he knows who you will meet in the future!

You are stronger than you think you are!

Believe God and realize that you are stronger than you think you are! I am a witness that when I was being traumatized by the enemy to the point of exhaustion, I had to remember the promises in the Word of God about trials! In other words, I realized that if God allowed the storm to come, I already had what I needed to survive it. The Bible says in **1 Corinthians 10:13,**

"There have no temptation taken you, but such as is common to man: but God is faithful, who will not suffer you to be tempted above that ye are able; but will with the temptation also make a way to escape, that ye may be able to bear it." In the English, the word temptation means, enticement or allurement especially to evil. This English definition is limited so we'll look at it in the Greek.

In the Greek, the word temptation is the word **peirasmos** which means, a putting to proof; provocation; adversity; to try; test or scrutinize. According to this definition, the word temptation written in this scripture, **1 Corinthians 10:13** means no sin, test or trial will be able to destroy you, **if** you stay with God. That's the key: Stay with God no matter what you go through. Praise the Lord!

If you are currently suffering, and it looks like the pain will never stop, understand that every trial has an ending date! Though if feels like its never-ending, don't trust that feeling and don't believe the lies from the devil! You will come out even stronger than you were before the trial started. When God sees that you've had enough and you've learned the intended lesson, he will command the storm in your life to stop! It is his promise to us. I can testify that he will deliver you, right on time! When my burdens got too heavy, I had to remind myself of the truth and authority of **1 Corinthians 10:13.** In other words, many times I had to encourage myself that my God would deliver me! It may sound strange, but I had to focus on the facts that God had not forgotten me and that he would come to my rescue! I came out of every storm stronger, better and graced with wisdom. I've been able to use these experiences to help other people who were going through similar problems.

When you are going through a bombardment of assaults and don't know what to do, get some help from a minister or a professional counselor, a trusted family member or a wise friend. Please know that you do not have to suffer in silence. Get help when you need it! It's perfectly okay to reach out for guidance and support when necessary. If fact, it is the healthy thing to do for your mental and emotional well-being. Above all else, pray and ask God for help. The Bible says in **1 Peter 5:7, "Cast your cares upon him, because he cares for you."** Some situations are just too heavy for you to carry alone. Give it to the Lord as you navigate through the issues of life. Do what you can do, but allow God to be in control of your life. He really does care for you!

At the end of the day, it's your life. You have the power to make intelligent decisions that will help you pursue your aspirations and accomplish your goals. You can decide to be at peace and happy in this life. The question is, who did you give away your power to make and keep you happy? You are not what you've been through. You are unique, and you were formed and designed with purpose. God is concerned that you are morally developed and that you reach your full potential. Every situation that you experience should be used to help positively mature your mental, personal and spiritual growth. Don't dwell on bad experiences by allowing them to make you bitter, but use them to help make you a better person. You can and will make it to the other side of every traumatic trial. You will be a better person, because you chose to keep living and to press through to a victorious conclusion.

Let's review a familiar story in the Bible of Daniel, who was placed in a lion's den because he disobeyed the king's decree that the people were not to pray. Daniel decided to obey God. He went home, opened his windows and prayed just like he had always done. He defied the king's written decree and was thrown into the lions' den **(Daniel 6:10**). Historically, those lions were literally starved for five days when prisoners were scheduled to be executed via this savage method. This mistreatment of the animals was to ensure that they were extremely hungry and angry. Their deprived condition guaranteed that they would immediately attack and viciously devour the human prey that was thrown into the pit. Daniel was thrown into the pit and the angry, starved lions looked at Daniel, their potential feast, but the lions never opened their mouths to kill Daniel! This defies logic or reasoning. It was a miracle!

You may feel like you're in an impossible, negative situation with wicked acting people who are attacking you with their words at every turn. What they try to use to harm you will not work! Just like angels stopped the mouths of the lions from hurting or killing Daniel, God can stop the mouths of your enemies from killing your reputation! The Bible says in **Isaiah 54:17, "No weapon that is formed against thee shall prosper; and every tongue that shall rise against thee in judgment thou shalt condemn. This is the heritage of the servants of the Lord, and their righteousness is of me, says the Lord."** People may come against you, but their tricks and schemes will not work! They will not destroy you!

You will survive the temptation, trial or test in your life, but you will also thrive! What does it mean to thrive? Thriving is characterized by success and prosperity after a setback or negative situation. It means to be victorious rather than being defeated, with a victim's mentality. As you heal from the trauma that you have suffered, you will come to a place of victory and begin to prosper in life. Prosperity means financial, mental and physical health, abundance and blessings!

As you recover from setbacks and continue walking on the journey of life, learn how to surround yourself with people who celebrate you. Spend your quality time with individuals who appreciate the precious jewel that you are. You deserve a life full of happiness and joy which comes from God who gives you the strength to live this life. The Word declares in **Nehemiah 8:10, "...The joy of the Lord is your strength."** That is your birthright as a Christian! Though you may be going through a host of problems and you may experience sad situations, you will have happy days again. Remember, no problem lasts forever! Until the trial ends, let your joy be renewed through your faith in God's restorative power! Fully decide to allow God to be the head of your life as you follow his guidance. Keep the lines of communication open between you and the Lord Jesus Christ through prayer, praise and thanksgiving for all that God has planned for you. Make the decisions necessary to choose the best options for your life. Though you will have trials and you might have to cry sometimes, the trial will not last forever. Remember, the Bible says in **Proverbs 30:5, "…Weeping may endure for a night, but joy comes in the morning."** Please say out loud, "My morning is coming!" Praise the Lord!

The Choice to Rejoice

As you make the choice to live your best life, exclude people from your inner circle who mistreat you or disrespect you. Individuals who truly love you will respect and value you; therefore, they will treat you right! You can and must choose to have joy again which means to Rejoice! We are enthusiastically encouraged to rejoice in **Philippians 4:4, "Rejoice in the Lord always: and again, I say Rejoice."**

You were made in the very image of God and he wants you to live a peaceful, joyful and fulfilled or satisfying life. The Lord doesn't want you depressed. You have every right to be happy in this life. Jesus said in **John 10:10, "…I came that you might have life and that more abundantly."** When you are just barely existing and not living a happy, satisfied and fulfilled life, you are living beneath your privileges! Arise and live your best life with those who cherish and celebrate you! Your time on this earth is measured and precious: therefore, share your life with family and friends who enhance and bless you, just as you are a blessing to others. My sisters and brothers, press through to the joy and happiness that you deserve! The decision is up to you! I decree and declare that you truly can, **Rejoice After Rejection! Hallelujah!**

God's Plan of Salvation:

God loves you and he wants a relationship with you. He sent his son Jesus to die for your sins. The Bible says in **John 3:16, "For God so loved the world that he gave his only begotten Son, that whosoever believeth in him should not perish, but have everlasting life."** The phrase believeth in him (Jesus) means to trust and lean on him. God made a way for you to live for and walk with him, as you live your life.

Prayer to give your life to God through Jesus:

God, I have sinned in my life and I'm sorry for the wrong I've done. I ask that you forgive me and change me. Help me live a life that pleases you. I believe that Jesus Christ is the Son of God and I accept him as my Lord and Savior. Wash me with the precious Blood of Jesus Christ, which was shed for my sins. Deliver me from all unrighteousness and sin, and help me to live for you, in Jesus' name, Amen.

After the Prayer:

If you sincerely prayed the above prayer, you are saved. The Bible says in **Romans 10:9, "If you will confess with your mouth the Lord Jesus and believe in your heart that God raised him from the dead, you will be saved."** Join and faithfully attend a good Bible believing, teaching church. Start reading you Bible every day or as often as you can. The New Testament would be a great place to start. Remember to pray, which is simply communication with God the Father, Jesus Christ the Son of God, and the Holy Ghost or Holy Spirit. Praise God every day, because he is worthy of your praise! The Bible says in **Psalm 150:6, "Let everything that has breath, praise the Lord! Praise the Lord!"** Sincerely serve the Lord Jesus Christ and grow spiritually through the grace of God! Be Blessed!

About the Author

Permetrice Milroe Jackson is an author of two intriguing novels. The latest is entitled *Duplicity: Double Life Drama*, which is available in Kindle, Nook and paperback formats. She also wrote the inspirational booklet, *Effective Prayers in Jesus' Name* which is also available in Kindle, Nook, ITunes/IBooks.com and paperback formats. She is a minister of the Gospel and a seasoned conference and revival speaker. Permetrice is a poet who is often asked to write original poems for various Christian services and other social events. She is an actress and has performed in plays in Atlanta, Georgia. Permetrice has been interviewed on various cable programs such as Atlanta's TV57 WATC, *Atlanta Live Program* and local broadcast news channel FOX 5 Atlanta.

Permetrice has a Bachelor of Arts Degree in Business Administration with a Concentration in Marketing from Clark Atlanta University in Atlanta, Georgia. She had an illustrious career with the Federal Government, Department of the Army, where she personally worked with active duty, two and three-star army generals, teaching them various computer skills as well as the use of other technology equipment. Permetrice served as a Division Chief and supervised military officers and enlisted soldiers. She traveled extensively across the Southeast United States to support 72 subordinate offices, ensuring procedural compliance with federal regulations. Permetrice also conducted automation and communications inspections at various military installations. She resigned to pursue her dreams of devoting more time with her children and she later answered the call to evangelistic ministry.

Permetrice Milroe Jackson is currently a highly qualified, certified high school teacher. She loves motivating her students to work hard and to make great decisions so that they develop into life-long learners who are academically and personally ready for college, professional careers, entrepreneurship and successful lives.

Permetrice has a passion for reading and she loves to write. She is currently writing two additional novels and several inspirational books.

To contact the author for speaking engagements, send correspondence to the address of the publisher or you may contact her at pmjatlanta@yahoo.com. Permetrice Milroe Jackson would love for you to follow her on Twitter and Instagram @pmjatlanta.